Made in God's Image to Live for His Glory

Embracing Your Creative Purpose

By Jocelyn Whitfield

Copyright © 2011 by Jocelyn Whitfield

Made in God's Image to Live for His Glory
Embracing Your Creative Purpose
by Jocelyn Whitfield

Printed in the United States of America

ISBN 9781613793527

All rights reserved solely by the author. The author guarantees all contents are original and do not infringe upon the legal rights of any other person or work. No part of this book may be reproduced in any form without the permission of the author. The views expressed in this book are not necessarily those of the publisher.

Unless otherwise indicated, Bible quotations are taken from New International version, Copyright © 1973, 1978, 1984 by Biblica Inc. and The Message. Copyright © 1993, 1994, 1995, 1996, 2000, 2001, 2002 by NavPress Publishing Group. All rights reserved. Used by permission.

www.xulonpress.com

Acknowledgements

I dedicate this book to my parents, who are at home with the Lord but who introduced me to the love of Christ, prayer, and God's word. Also, to my son, Aaron, who has enriched my life and given me so much joy. I wait patiently to see God's purpose unfold fully in your life.

I am grateful to my siblings, who have been my best friends, as we have together been able to share the blessing of knowing Christ. To my nieces, cousins, mentees, and friends, thank you for allowing me to share my faith and my love of God with you. To my teachers and pastors, thank you for shaping my life and imparting to me words of wisdom and truth.

I am most thankful to Dr. Frederick K. Price and the ministry staff of Crenshaw Christian Center for giving me a thirst for God's Word and playing a vital role in my discipleship and growing my faith. Also, a special thanks to my pastor and friend Dr. David Anderson, Pastor of Bridgeway Community Church, for broadening my perspective on the extravagant generosity of God's grace; and for allowing us to see God's grace at work in his life, the life of the church and in each of us.

I am also so very thankful to God for the gift of June Mickens. Thanks for your editorial assistance with this project. Thank you for being a gentle, but an incredible, value added to my life.

FOREWORD
by Dr. David A. Anderson

Can you hear it? I can hear it loud and clear. It is the sound of Jocelyn Whitfield's passion to teach and preach God's word about the victorious Christian life that is possible for all of us. As you read each chapter, Jocelyn's passion and heart of care leaps off every page with hope, insight, and inspiration.

My wife and I have sat at Jocelyn's feet to hear her speak life into us on more than one occasion. The bible says, "The tongue has the power of life and death and those who love it will eat its fruit." (Proverbs 18:21) Jocelyn's pen will provide you much fruit to eat. If you adhere to the words on the pages in front of you, you will be sustained spiritually and be encouraged personally. My prayer is that Jocelyn's words will bear much fruit in your lives as they have borne much fruit in mine.

The prophetic word of faith in Jocelyn's life has been a witness to me and others at Bridgeway Community Church in Columbia, Maryland and has lifted our gaze from what is to what can be. I couldn't be more grateful for the work in my personal life and the work in the kingdom of God that Jocelyn has accomplished through her spirit of faith and her love for the Lord.

Contents

Introduction xi

Chapter 1 The Extravagant Generosity of God's Grace: Knowing God Personally and Intimately 13

Chapter 2 The Gift of Prayer: Communing and Fellowshipping with Our Heavenly Father 18

Chapter 3 Finding the Real Life in God's Word 25

Chapter 4 Embracing the God Kind of Life: Walking by Faith 31

Chapter 5 Becoming a True Worshipper: Fulfilling God's Creative Purpose 41

Chapter 6 The Abundant Life: Obedience and Victory over Sin 48

Chapter 7 Welcome Holy Spirit: My Friend, Advocate, and Revealer of Truth 54

Chapter 8 Loving the Way God Loves 60

Chapter 9 Living for His Glory 67

Poem 73

References 75

Notes 81

Introduction

I started writing this book about nine years ago. It wasn't until recently that I felt prompted by the Holy Spirit to finish it. God's timing is always right, and His seasons are always perfect. I now am in a season of life in which years are quickly passing. As we grow older, we tend to examine our lives and actions more carefully in view of God's purpose and plans. We want to ensure that everything that we do for God reflects who He is, reveals His divine purpose, and brings Him glory. As the years fade, we come to understand our creative purpose. We have been *"Made in God's Image to Live for His Glory"* (Isaiah 43:7).

There are no greater purposes in life than living for and reflecting God's glory; displaying His goodness, mercy, splendour, love, holiness, and excellence; manifesting His beauty; making His Name known; and sharing in His praise. Because of Christ, our Savior and Lord, and the generosity of His grace, we have been afforded the enormous honor of bearing His image on earth. God loved us so much that He gave us the best of His riches, His Son, Jesus the Christ. The blood of His Son was poured on the altar of sacrifice so that we could reflect His glory. It was a lavish sacrifice – costly, extravagant, and expensive. However, He deemed us worth it. In Christ, we now have the capacity to reflect the glory and radiance of the

Father just as Jesus did (Hebrews 1:3); to put on His character, value, and worth; and to manifest His presence to the world.

Because we are in Christ, we are not like others who are without hope or a purpose. Christ is our hope of glory, and because He abides in us, we are filled with the glory of God. We do not have to wander through this life without a purpose or destination. Our purpose and destination are sure. We have been created to bear forth the image of our God and to display His glory and His goodness to the world. We have been called to share the good news, to make Christ and His attributes known, and lead the praise of His Name.

In the chapters that follow, I will share some of the foundational truths that have transformed my life. These truths have been the bedrocks of my spiritual development and maturity. In these chapters, you will get a glimpse of His work in my life and how through prayer, faith, love, worship, obedience, the Word, and the precious Holy Spirit, I have strived, and continue to strive, to live a life that glorifies Him. Please know that I have not arrived yet at the destination that God has in mind for me, but also know that each day I am praying that His glory will be revealed in me.

It is my prayer that, as you read each page of this book, your knowledge and understanding of God will increase and that your heart will be set free to please Him. I also pray that you will not just be motivated to understand how Christ lived but that you will be compelled and determined to be satisfied with nothing less than to bring glory to the chief architect of our lives, our Father and God.

Chapter 1

The Extravagant Generosity of God's Grace: Knowing God Personally and Intimately

For, after all, put it as we may to ourselves, we are all of us from birth to death guests at a table which we did not spread. The sun, the earth, love, friends, our very breath are parts of the banquet.... Shall we think of the day as a chance to come nearer to our Host, and to find out something of Him who has fed us so long? ~Rebecca Harding Davis

God desires that we know Him personally and intimately. Through our Lord and Savior, Jesus Christ, we have been given the privilege to know Him. God has pursued, and continues to pursue, a loving and personal relationship with each one of us. He created us and knows us. He even knows each strand of hair on our head. He wants us to know Him and His heart and to understand His ways. He wants to be in fellowship with us and to give us meaning and purpose for our lives.

All human beings are born with the desire to know their creator, even though they may not acknowledge Him as God. This is why we see people seeking spiritual advisors, astrologers, psychics, and other gods. They want someone or something to give them insight about their purpose and future. No matter how much these sought-after individuals and so called *gods* tell them, though, they later discover that these are only temporary fixes – misleading and not to be depended on for the long term.

In reality, there is no one who can tell us as much about ourselves as our Heavenly Father, our Creator. He is all knowledgeable. There is an old saying, which is still true today, "We all need to know God for ourselves." Our mothers', fathers', and even the preachers' knowledge of God can only provide us with inspiration for knowing Him or give us knowledge regarding Him. However, relationship with God must be personal; substitutes are not allowed. Isn't it wonderful to know that God wants a personal and intimate relationship with each one of us? He has paved the path, through the blood of Jesus, so that we can know Him. Jesus said that this is eternal life that we know the only true God and Jesus Christ whom God has sent (John 17:3).

God says in the book of Jeremiah:

"Let not the wise and skillful person glory and boast in his wisdom and skill; let not the mighty and powerful person glory and boast in his strength and power; let not the person who is rich [in physical gratification and earthly wealth] glory and boast in his [temporal satisfactions and earthly] riches; But let him who glories glory in this: that he understands and knows Me [personally and practically, directly discerning and recognizing My character],

that I am the Lord, Who practices loving-kindness, judgment, and righteousness in the earth, for in these things I delight," says the Lord. (Jeremiah 9:23, 24 Amplified)

God desires that we have a faithful, loving, and covenant relationship with Him. Think about the covenant relationship of a husband and wife. As that relationship matures, something amazing happens; they begin to know each other's thoughts and ways. They become intimately acquainted with each other and responsive to each other's needs. Similarly, as we enter into a relationship and union with Christ, we become much like a married couple. In this covenant, loving, and faithful relationship, we draw close to God, and He draws close to us. We begin to take on His thoughts and ways, and we begin to know the immeasurable and unlimited surpassing greatness of His power in us and for us.

Throughout the Bible we see God seeking a covenant relationship with His people and revealing faithfulness and love to them. Of all the patriarchs of the Bible, I believe that King David had one of the clearest views of God and who He is. David lived in a vibrant, trusting, affectionate, and reverent relationship with God. He not only loved God, but he sought His wisdom, presence, and intervention in every aspect of his life. David's determined purpose was that he would let nothing separate him from the love and presence of God, not even his sin. In response, God revealed Himself to David in many ways. He became David's protector, defender, abundant provider, ever-lasting Father, and his faithful friend.

As God revealed Himself to David, He also revealed Himself to others. For instance, in Genesis, He reveals Himself as Elohim – the Creator (Genesis 1:1); Jehovah – our eternal God, the Almighty God, full of life, greatness, glory, power, and creative ability (Genesis 2:4); El Shaddai – the many breasted one, the all-sufficient one, the one who satisfies and multiplies, full of might, nourishment, and bounty (Genesis 17:1-2); as Adonai, Abraham's Lord and Master (Genesis 15:2); and as Jehovah-Jireh, the Lord who sees and provides (Genesis 22:1-19). In Exodus, He reveals Himself as Jehovah-Nissi, the protector, deliverer, the God of miracles and victories (Exodus 17:15); and as Jehovah-Rapha, the great physician, who heals physically and emotionally (Exodus 15:22-27). These are but a few examples of God's character, nature, and His love for His people.

Throughout the Bible, we see that God reveals His covenant relationship to His people in many ways. I encourage you to study the Names of God fully. In your study, you will discover a God who is passionately concerned about the welfare of His people. The Names of God reveal who He is in relation to us. It is undisputable that God always has loved His people and has wanted to be involved in their lives and to do them good. Nothing has changed; He still desires to reveal Himself to us. Today, He reveals Himself to us through His Son, Jesus.

Knowing God intimately and personally is the greatest privilege in life. Real contentment and joy can only come from knowing Him. There is nothing more important, no greater priority, and nothing in life as valuable and precious.

> *Dear Father,*
>
> *My heart longs to know you, not just to be acquainted with you or to have a brief encounter, but to have an intimate relationship with you. I want to be more than your child; I want to be your friend. When people see me, I want them say that I walk, talk, and live like Christ. Father, I thank you for making me in Your image and likeness so that the world can know you. I thank you for making this possible through Jesus. Show me how to glorify you and to do what is pleasing in your sight. It's in the Name of Jesus that I pray. Amen*

Chapter 2

The Gift of Prayer: Communing and Fellowshipping with Our Heavenly Father

Walking with God down the avenue of prayer we acquire something of His likeness, and unconsciously we become witnesses to others of His beauty and His grace. ~ E. M. Bounds

Prayer is a gracious gift, honor, and privilege. It is the most vital practice and at the core of our personal relationship with God. It is one of the ways that we communicate and fellowship with our Heavenly Father and invite Him to be involved in our daily lives. In our conversations with the Father, we hear His voice; our desires are declared; and our hope is restored. Forgiveness is given; grace is imparted; dependence on God is realized; and our trust and faith in Him is strengthened. It is a time of fellowship, friendship, and intimacy with our Lord. It is about talking *and* listening. It is about knowing that God is aware of everything that we are experiencing and that He is present to hear and respond.

Prayer isn't about our posture – the way we sit, stand, or kneel. It isn't about our location; prayer can happen anywhere – in a car, lying on the bed, walking the streets. God is everywhere, and His Spirit lives in us.

Prayer isn't about grammar or a particular way the words should be enunciated. It can be as simple as a whispered "Help me Lord," or it can follow the pattern that was given us in the Lord's Prayer (Matthew 6:9-13). In fact, we do not have to depend on ourselves for the words at all; the Holy Spirit, who abides in us, gives us the right words to pray. He comes alongside us, helping us to say what it is in our hearts. If we do not know how to pray or what to pray in certain circumstances, it doesn't matter. He will do the praying for us and through us with wordless signs and aching groans. He knows us far better than we know ourselves. He knows our condition and keeps us present before God. That's why we can be sure that every detail in our lives God works together for our good (Romans 8:26-28).

At an early age, I was introduced to prayer. It always has been a practice and discipline of mine and my family. I can vividly remember the prayer meetings that occurred in my home growing up. On Sunday mornings, my father gathered us around the bed, and we got on our knees for a time of prayer. He would ask God to bless his children's coming in and going out and to open doors for us that no man would be able to close. I can hear my father as if it were today. I did not know that he had memorized and was reciting Scripture from Deuteronomy 28, but I did know that God honored my father's prayers.

My mother was also a person of much prayer. Because of her illness, she tended to pray quietly in her bedroom, but she prayed about everything and everyone. People were always coming to our house for prayer, even pastors. On some level, she may have missed that my mother believed in the power of prayer for everyone but herself. You may be asking how this could be. However, this happens to many of us. While we can believe God to answer prayers for others, it is often hard to believe that God will answer our prayers for us. I think that's what happened with my mother. Because of this I think my mother missed the great blessing of seeing God's amazing work in her own personal life.

I remember Wednesday night prayer in our home. Members of the church, family, and friends would come to our house to pray for the needs of the church and its families. We would all stand in a circle as people petitioned God to respond to the many needs that were spoken. Testimonies were shared about answered prayer. Tears of joy were expressed, as person after person was touched by the Spirit of the Lord. In the circle, we experienced the love of God and trusted that our needs were, or would be, met. These were wonderful times of fellowship in our household, and the atmosphere was filled with the presence of the Lord.

King David, one my favorite heroes of the Bible, was a man of prayer and worship. David freely exercised this gift and privilege of prayer. He made few decisions without seeking counsel, wisdom, direction, and guidance from God (1 Samuel 30:7-8). David did not rely on his own wisdom, ability, and capacity but on the power and presence of God. It was the key to David's successes. He understood that His blessings and victories were connected to having a fluid relationship with the Lord and being obedient to Him. We can be confident in God's faithfulness, if we follow David's example of prayer. What has been will be again; what has been done will be done again.

Perhaps our best example of prayer is Jesus himself. Christ prayed and established a model for us. In the Scriptures, it is not uncommon to find Christ leaving His disciples and going off to a solitary place to pray. Sometimes He spent nights in prayer.

He also instructed and taught His disciples to pray. In Matthew 6, Jesus established a pattern and process for prayer. The one thing that is so fascinating about this prayer, which has come to be known as *The Lord's Prayer*, is that it is personal and relational. In this prayer, first and foremost, Jesus establishes our relationship with God; He is our Father. Next, we learn that His Name is to be hallowed and honored. Then come repentance, having our daily needs met, and deliverance from the evil one. Finally, we are reminded that, though God is our Father, He also is God; He has rules over all, has all power, and deserves all glory.

While Jesus set a pattern for prayer, we are not locked into that prayer or that format. God really just wants you to communicate with Him, and there are various ways that we can do that.

One way to pray is by praying God's word. In order to do this, we need to know the promises of God and what He says about our situations and circumstances. The Bible is the most useful tool for this.

In the Bible, we will find the promises of God and the provisions that He has made for us through His word. Search your concordance for the topics that cover your situation. Meditate on these Scriptures, and then begin to personalize them. For example, if you are fearful, you may say, "I thank you, God, that you have not given me the spirit of fear but of power, love, and a sound mind." (2 Timothy 1:7 KJV)

When we pray God's word, faith and power are released in us to believe. Hebrews 4:12 says that God's word is alive and powerful, sharper than a two-edged sword. When we speak and pray the Scriptures, we are coming into agreement with God. We are putting His words into our hearts and affirming what He says. In other words, confessing His word and saying what He says activates our faith because faith comes by hearing and hearing by the word of God (Romans 10:17). When we confess God's word, we are not trying to convince God to do anything; we are growing our faith. God responds to His word and our faith. Scripture tells us that His words cannot return to Him void of action (Isaiah 55:11); they must accomplish what He has sent them to do. God can never go against His words. By speaking God's promises, His word, we are praying the answer, rather than focusing on the problem. In doing this, we give God the opportunity to perform His word in our lives and to make good on His promises. Jeremiah 1:12 states that God watches over His word to perform it. God's words are spirit and life, and that life comes to fruition in the spoken word. God's word in the Bible can have power only because it corresponds to God's word in the universe. It is the present voice, which makes the written word powerful. Otherwise, it would lay locked in slumber within the covers of a book.

Equally as important for effective prayer is the authority that we have been given by Jesus to use His Name in prayer (Mark 16:17-18; John 14:14). Jesus said that whatever we ask in His Name, He will do, so that the Father may be glorified in the Son (John 14:13) and whatever we ask the Father in His Name, He will give us (John 16:23). God has highly exalted Jesus and has given Him a Name that is above every name (Philippians 2:9). There is no other Name by which we can saved (Acts 4:12 & 10:43; 1 John 2:12). Accordingly, we can pray to the Father, in the

Name of Jesus, and know that we will get a response because of what Jesus has done for us.

It is important that we understand and know the power behind the Name of Jesus. It is not a magical name that we add to the beginning and ending of our prayers hoping that God will do something. It is the Name above every name, and there is no other name in heaven or earth that has been given such honor. There will come a point in time when everything and everybody, whether in heaven or earth, will have to bow to that Name (Philippians 2:10). No other name will give us access to the throne of grace. Because of the wonderful Name of Jesus, we can boldly enter the throne room of God and receive mercy and favor in our time of need (Hebrews 4:16).

Prayer is one of God's most generous grace gifts. You have not done, and never will do, anything that makes you worthy of this gift. It is given just because God loves you and wants to be in fellowship with you. You do not have to be a gifted orator to pray, nor do you have to be an adult to pray. This gift is given to His children, regardless of race or ethnicity, age, gender, or status in the community or the church. If anyone has accepted Christ as Savior, God hears his prayers. And, for anyone who has not chosen to follow Christ, God promises to hear a sinner's repentant prayer and to welcome you from death into life, from exclusion to inclusion in the family of faith. When we receive and accept this gift of prayer, we can enter into the glorious presence of our Father.

Dear Father,

Teach me how to pray and communicate with you. Let not a day go by without my talking with you. Give me attentive ears that I might listen and hear you speak so that I may live my life pleasing to you. Give me wisdom, insight and answers to issues I face. I'll not forget to hallow your Name and to give you thanksgiving and praise even before your answer is revealed. Help me remember that the power to live this life comes from my communion with you. It's in the Name of Jesus, the Christ, the Anointed One, I pray. Amen

Chapter 3

Finding the Real Life in God's Word

The Bible is not an end in itself, but a means to bring men to an intimate and satisfying knowledge of God, that they may enter into Him, that they may delight in His Presence, may taste and know the inner sweetness of the very God Himself in the core and center of their hearts. ~ A. W. Tozer

As a child needs milk or food to live daily, every believer must have a regular measure of the word of God to grow spiritually and to live abundantly and victoriously. Many of us are searching for direction and God's will in our lives. Often we go to others – counselors, preachers, friends – attempting to find an answer to our problems. Not that this is wrong or cannot help, but I have found that the best counsel we can receive comes from the word of God. There is no substitute for the word of God. It is our blueprint and manual for living. It is a lamp for our feet and a light for our path. It shows us the way and keeps us from wandering off the path designed for us by God. Let me tell you; if you are trying to live this Christian life with only a Sunday dose of the word of God from your preacher, you're in trouble. We need the word of God to sustain us daily. It holds us up, keeps us, carries us, nurtures us, nourishes us, and preserves us through the good and bad times.

God's words are not ordinary words; they are alive, God-breathed, and supernatural. The words of God are His voice. They have been given to us so that we can fully and completely live for God and do what He has called us to do. The more we fill ourselves with His word, the more we gain spiritual insight and wisdom for living successful lives – lives that are pleasing to God.

God's word is our only surety. It will never return unto Him void; in short, God's words cannot come back empty-handed. So, when we speak His word, we have the surety that it will accomplish what God said it would. Every word of God is foolproof and backed up by Him. He makes good on His promises and will fulfill them (Isaiah 44:24-26). Jesus said, "Man does not live by bread alone, but by every word that comes from the mouth of God." (Matthew 4:4) The word is living, powerful, and sharper than a sword; it penetrates even marrow and bone and is a discerner of the thoughts and intents of the heart (Hebrews 4:12). It has the capacity and power to renew our bodies, souls, and minds and to bring healing to our physical bodies.

When I was young, my parents insisted that we memorized Scripture. Whether it was in a room on our knees or around the dinner table, all the siblings were required to quote a Scripture. Both of my parents were people who loved God's word, but my father taught me early on that the only sure thing that I could rely on was the word of God. For all of my father's adult life, he memorized Scripture, and for years, I thought my father was an avid Bible reader because each time He prayed He recited

Scripture. It wasn't until I was in college that I discovered the truth. When my father went back to school to get his GED, I learned that he struggled with reading and writing and that my mother did most of his reading and writing for him. You see, when he was a young boy, his father died. My father quit school at age 10 to take care of his mother and siblings. Despite this handicap, my father was able to master many jobs and even rose to a supervisory capacity. He was a keen listener, had an incredible memory, and would memorize what He heard. That was true at work and at home. Because he memorized Bible verses so cleverly and was able to recite them verbatim, no one ever knew that he had reading problems. My father hid God's words in His heart, and they were alive to and in him.

My mother was also a lover of God's word. Reading the Bible was her first love. I often found her sitting on the side of the bed with her glasses on her nose, thumbing through the word of God. She studied and searched the Scripture daily, underlining passages. My mother was bedridden for many years, suffering from rheumatoid arthritis and in pain. Her fingers were quite deformed; she could barely bend them to hold the pencil to underline the passages in her Bible or to write them down. No matter how severe the pain, though, she believed God's word and would say that He is a faithful and loving God. When I would come home from college, my mother and I would read the Bible together. She often sat me on her bed and reminded me of God's promises. She knew that I was concerned about her health. She knew that my faith was being shaken. However, she often told me that, if God chose not to heal her physical body in this life, she was assured that He would give her a glorified body in the life to come. Until my mother's passing, she relied on God's word.

She did not see her health restored in this life, but she held on to God's word, and I'm sure she's rejoicing over her glorified body today.

My mother was my hero – a woman of prayer, faith, and the word. She was a wonderful mentor to me as well as to our neighbors. I remember days coming home to find our neighbors sitting around her bed studying God's word. It didn't matter what they believed, she would share the word of God with them. During the last two years of my mother's life, she sold light bulbs over the phone. It wasn't that she needed the money, but it gave her the opportunity to minister and tell others about Jesus. Many men and women received Christ through this ministry.

At my mother's funeral, people from far and near and from various ethnicities came to celebrate her homecoming. They shared with the family the impact that my mother had on their lives. They talked about her studying the Bible with them and praying for them. Yes, this woman, my mother, led hundreds of people to the Lord, I believe, simply because she was in love with God's word and wanted others to know this Savior that she loved. It was the word that kept her alive as long as she lived. She kept it close by her side on that small table in front of her bed. I do not think it was ever out of her sight. My mother's Bible never needed dusting. She used it daily, and it was life to her. Each word she took in was God-breathed, giving her strength and power to live each day.

Many of us are healthy and may not have deformities like my mother's, but yet we leave the most precious book in life untouched on our coffee tables catching dust. The words in the Bible contain vital nutrients to our spiritual life, growth, and success. Psalm 1:2-3 says that blessed is the man who delights in God's word and meditates (chews on it) on it day and night; he will be like a tree, firmly planted by the streams of water, that yields fruit in its season, that has leaves that don't wither, and that prospers in whatever he does. God told the Israelites, when they settled in Canaan, that their success and prosperity was dependent upon keeping the word of God in their mouths, meditating on it day and night, and doing what it says (Joshua 1:8). The word of God has the explicit power to prepare and equip us for every good work. It is profitable for teaching, for reproof, for correction, and for training in righteousness (2 Timothy 3:16, 17).

Interesting, the Bible also is esteemed by many non-believers. For many centuries, it has been used as a model for human behavior and morality. Most of the laws and regulations in our country and other nations have been adapted from the Ten Commandments and the other guidelines that God gave to Moses and shared with us in Exodus and Leviticus. Because of the veracity and fidelity of the Bible, people testifying in our court systems are asked to swear by it. If even unbelievers adhere to the guidance found in the Bible, shouldn't we, as believers, immerse ourselves in the word of God in order to learn about our God, how to live, and who we are in Christ? Shouldn't we receive God's word, not just as words of men, but as God's word and truth? Shouldn't we allow the word of God to do its effective work in us and to wash us clean daily? If we hide the word in our hearts and let it flow from our mouths, we will become living epistles, written by the Spirit of God and both known and read by men (2 Corinthians 3:2-3). We will become His letters to a dying world, reflecting His glory, His goodness, and His mercy.

> *Father,*
>
> *Order my steps in your word. Your words are lights to my path. They give direction and guide me into truth. I do not want to disobey your words but to the delight in them. Keep your words in my mouth for they are life and health to me. They empower me and give me hope. Help me to remember your Name that I may keep your words. Do well unto me, Lord, as I honor your word, and help me to keep your words in my heart so that I will not sin against you. It is in the Name of Jesus, the Christ. Amen*

Chapter 4

Embracing the God Kind of Life: Walking by Faith

Faith isn't the ability to believe long and far into the misty future. It's simply taking God at His Word and taking the next step. ~Joni Eareckson Tada

You may have heard the Joni Eareckson Tada story. She was paralyzed from the neck down after a serious diving accident. Though disabled, Joni did not stop pursuing God's purpose for her life. She now has a ministry helping the disabled. She is a minister, noted author, artist, and wife. To me, Joni is one of our greatest examples of a person of faith. She moved beyond her physical limitations to glorify God. She has been able to accomplish more than you and I can imagine because she believes God has a special purpose for her life. Because of the faith given by God, Joni has been able to do exceedingly abundantly above anything that we could fathom. But, the amazing news is that God is no respecter of persons. We all have been given varying measures of that faith (Romans 12:3).

Friends used to ask me whether I was one of those "Faith Believers." My answer has always been the same. Yes. I am a daughter of faith, and every believer should be a child of faith. Our very salvation is based on the measure of faith given us. When the gospel was preached, we heard the word and responded in faith, repented of our sins, and asked Jesus to come into our hearts. Our hearts were supernaturally transformed, and we acknowledged Jesus as our Messiah. A Christian's faith starts and ends with God. God calls us into a confident assurance and trust in His ability to deliver on what He has promised. God requires His children to come to Him in faith, believing that He rewards those who diligently seek Him. Without faith, it is impossible to please Him (Hebrews 11:6). Hebrews 11:1 states, "Now faith is the substance of things hoped for, the evidence of things not seen." The word of God is the substance that we hold onto, even when we do not have physical proof. The word becomes our deed, the assurance that God is faithful and able to perform His promises.

Faith is simply taking God at His word and being convinced that it is true. God has complete and perfect confidence in His power and ability to bring to pass that which He says or promises. Therefore, we too should be assured that He is faithful and able to perform His promises. What we feel has nothing to do with faith. It is not dependent upon our five physical senses – what we see, feel, taste, touch, or hear – or on our knowledge, or on our present and past experiences. Faith is based on the word of God. It is stimulated, activated, and increased by two things – hearing and acting on the word of God. Romans 10:17 says that "faith comes by hearing, and hearing by the word of God." As much as hearing the word activates and builds our faith, unless we put action to what we have heard, nothing will happen. James puts it this way: just as the body, without food, is dead; so faith, without corresponding action, is dead and devoid of life (James 2:15-17).

When I look back on my life, faith always has been active at one level or another. It was active, even when I did not know what it meant. I remember when I had been accepted into college. I was thrilled and sad at the same time. My parents didn't have the money to send me off to college. I did know, however, about the power of prayer, and I knew, as my mother had told me, that all things were possible for God and that nothing was impossible with Him. So I got down on my knees and prayed. When August came, I still did not have the money, but I had an assurance on the inside that God was going to come through. I held onto God's word that nothing was impossible. I prayed every day, believing that somehow God would come through for me. The only substance that I had was the promise set out in Scripture that all things are possible to those that believe (Matthew 19:26; Philippians 4:23). I was expectant that God would show up on my behalf. And, He did. Two weeks before school opened, God showed up. I had more than enough to pay for my college tuition. From that time on, I knew that God would come through for me. I didn't realize at the time that I was acting on what I believed, and this indeed was faith.

It wasn't until I was about 25 years old that I was able to understand what faith is and is not. A girlfriend of mine invited me to Crenshaw Christian Center in Los Angeles. This was one of the life-changing periods for me. For the first time in my life, Christ became alive to me, and I realized that our God really is a faithful God. Through the teaching of Pastor Frederick Price, the foundation of faith was laid, and I began to believe God like never before. I realized that, without faith in God, I could never please Him. The more Pastor Price taught about faith, the more my faith grew. The more I heard the word, the more I wanted to hear the word. I would listen to his messages on faith over and over again, and I came to understand that faith was the gateway to accessing all that God has for us. Not only did I hear the word and put it in my heart, but I began to speak the word. I spoke it often because I realized that only God's words could penetrate my doubts and increase my faith. The more I spoke the word of God, the more I was assured of God's faithfulness.

It is God's desire that our faith will grow. As Christians, we are always facing new challenges. I believe this is why many heroes of the faith have what we call *ever-increasing faith*. Once God has responded to our faith for one thing, I guarantee you that we will be confronted with something larger to believe God for or to do.

Having sat under a modern-day giant of the faith, you would think it would have been easier for me to live by faith, but that wasn't always the case. To whom much is given, much is required (Luke 12:48). In other words, the more God gives you, the more He expects. As our faith increases, our challenges also may increase.

I remember when I returned to Maryland from California. I was assured that God had directed me to relocate. This wasn't something that I just came up with; there was a restlessness in my spirit until I said, "Yes." However, I was giving up my job and my worldly possessions to come to an area where I did not have a place to live and did not have a job, or even the prospect of one. All I had was what I believed God had spoken to me, a Scripture confirmation, and the counsel of friends.

I thought God was telling me to relocate because of personal reasons; however, I soon found out my personal reasons were not the whole of

God's plans for me. God had a greater plan in mind. His plan was not to bring any harm but to prosper me and to give me the hope and future that He had designed for me (Jeremiah 29:11).

So, I came to Baltimore with my son and little else, but knowing in my spirit that I had heard from God. Mind you, I said "in my spirit," not "in my mind." My mind kept telling me that I had made a mistake...and so did some my relatives. To them, this was not the time to relocate. It was during the Reagan Administration, and the economy was bad. Many people had been laid off, and jobs were scarce, but I was determined to believe God. If He didn't come through, then I was greatest fool in the world, and I guess my family would have been right in having me institutionalized.

After the move, money was scarce and almost running out, and employment still had not come, so I moved in with my cousin. What a blessing that was. But, what she didn't know was that every night, I comforted myself in God's word. I would speak God's words on prospering me. Every Scripture that I could find on employment and favor I packed into my heart and mouth. For 20 days, I confessed God's word about the situation and thanked God in anticipation of the job He was going to send. On the 21st day, something happened, but it wasn't what I expected. My aunt died. My father asked me to accompany him to the funeral in another state, which I did. While there, I got the chance to see a few cousins that I had not seen in years. I shared with them that I was seeking a job, and it turned out that one cousin knew the Personnel Director in Baltimore and promised to make a call on my behalf. That call resulted in an appointment and a referral to someone else, who referred me for a job at one of the Baltimore City hospitals. When all was said and done, I was offered a director's position. You can't believe the impact this had on my family and friends. They saw the God of miracles show up on behalf of His daughter. In a time of lack and impossibilities for most, God did what people thought was unconceivable – He granted me favor and provision. He was faithful to His word, and His word was alive. He said that He would never see those in right standing with Him (the righteous) forsaken or their children begging bread (Psalm 37:25), and my experience was living proof of that.

I did not know that, during this same time, God was opening the doors of ministry for me as well. All I knew was that I loved God and wanted to please Him. I knew that I could trust Him with my life. While I did not know much about ministry, I knew God had something more for me to do other than my professional career. While I was at Crenshaw Christian Center, I served on the personal ministry team. There, I experienced no greater joy than seeing people come to Christ. I knew that I was anointed to share with these individuals, and I rejoiced at the amazing spiritual transformation that took place as they gave their lives to Christ and received the Holy Spirit; even their faces seemed to glow. So, I knew that there was something for me to do for the Kingdom. I just didn't know what.

While in Baltimore working, I received an impression in my spirit, calling me to minister to women. "What does that mean? What am I supposed to do?" Well, as I prayed, I felt impressed to convene a Christian women's conference.

To be honest, I had never attended a Christian women's conference, much less hosted one. From what I could gather, during this period, there were very few of these conferences being done. In fact, I didn't even personally know of a women's ministry, except the one I had left back at Crenshaw. All I knew was prayer.

So I prayed and fasted, trying to get the mind of God on what He had called me to do. One day, sometime later, while watching TV, one of the commentators mentioned an event at the Baltimore Convention Center. Somehow, I knew that that was where the conference was to be held. However, with no money, how could I pay for a conference at the Baltimore Convention Center? Not only didn't I have money, but I didn't know anyone who could give me the money. In fact, the only two local people that I knew well were my cousin and best friend. Nonetheless, I scheduled an appointment with a sales representative at the Baltimore Convention Center. I told her what I had in mind and that I believed that God had called me to do this. (I was quite naïve about business at that time, though I was bold about my conviction in Christ.)

Can you believe that God orchestrated this meeting? The salesperson not only was a Christian but a minister of the gospel! God sent me to her and gave me favor with her. She promised to do whatever she could to help me, and together we prayed for the success of the event. She knew I didn't have any money, but yet she joined this faith walk with me. She was the angel that God sent me to carry out His will.

When asked how many people would be attending the event, my response was that I expected close to 1,000. Mind you, besides my cousin and best friend, I think I knew about five people in town at this stage. Though one of these people was a pastor, I am sure he thought I was deluded as I shared my vision for the conference.

To complicate matters, while planning the conference, I was laid off, which meant that my already limited financial resources were decreased even more. I had only a small unemployment check and a small IRS income tax return to work with. Clearly, there would have to be supernatural intervention by God because I already had signed a contract with the convention center. Despite being out of work, I continued to plan for the conference, believing that God would come through. I used my tax return to pay the deposit on the convention center, not knowing where the other money would come from. I continued believing in faith and praying that God would provide. Meanwhile, I had to begin securing speakers for the conference. Since I knew few people in Baltimore and did not know the churches or the first ladies, I was led to listen to Christian radio. From listening to radio, I was able to identify area churches as well as the pastors and their wives, and I was led to invite several women leaders to speak at the conference from various denominations and racial backgrounds.

The conference did happen, and it was one of the first for Baltimore. Close to 1,000 women attended, and God anointed and prospered the event. He not only showed up, but He showed out. How did this happen? I heard the voice of God. I acted on what He said. I held onto His word that He would prosper everything that I put my hand to (Psalm 1:3). I stood in faith, patiently expecting God to do what He had promised. Now I understand that, if I had not acted on God's word and followed His direction, women from churches of many denominations and of various races would not have come together to worship God; to learn about His plans for their lives; and, for some, to receive Christ as their Savior. God is faithful. He puts His faith into us so we can believe Him, and He backs it up by performing what He has promised.

Why is it that, at times, we do not receive after we have believed? Could it be that we lack patience? Often this is the case. Our timing is not always God's timing or His season. The greatest mistakes made in my life have happened because I lacked patience or because I wanted to help God resolve the problem or manifest the answer. Because I could not see it quickly, I lost faith and begin to fix the issue with my own natural abilities. Losing confidence can cost us. Scripture states that we are not to cast away our confidence, which has great reward; for we are in need of endurance (patience) so that, after we have done the will of God, we will see the promise (Hebrews 10:35-36). The truth is that we really don't need more faith; we need patience and simple belief that God's word is true. We have enough faith. God's faith is in us, and we can draw on it. Instead, we have to trust that our God will take care of us. In fact, in Scripture, Jesus tells us that, if we do not have that trusting faith like a child, then we cannot enter into the Kingdom of God (Matthew 18:2-4). The beginning of a life that is pleasing to God starts with child-like faith when we receive Christ as our Savior. As His children, we must garner a confident attitude toward God, believing that He is all-powerful and will act favorably in our lives.

To sum this up, if we do not operate in faith, God cannot have pleasure in us. He requires the just to live by faith and not to draw back. Jesus says that, if we embrace this God-life, nothing will be too much for us. We can tell a mountain to be removed, and it is as good as done (Matthew 17:20). With God, nothing is ever impossible, and no word from God shall be without power or possible fulfillment (Matthew 19:26). Without living this active and obedient life of faith, it is impossible to please God.

We have a great model of faith, and He is Jesus, the Christ. We can look up to Him because He is the author and finisher of our faith. He walked in obedient faith, even while enduring hardship. However, He persisted in His work, knowing that He would bring pleasure to His Heavenly Father. And, when we walk in faith, we follow Christ's example and bring pleasure to our God as well.

> *Father,*
>
> *Sometimes the circumstances of life seem to overwhelm me, and it is hard to believe that you will see me through. It isn't that I am faithless, but I am so accustomed to relying on my senses and natural abilities. Shower me with your mercy, and help me to take baby steps until my faith and trust in you increase. Help me not to look at my circumstances but at your greatness and your ability to bring those things that I desire to pass. Help me to look to Jesus, the author and finisher of my faith.*
>
> *Thank you, Lord!*
>
> *In the Name of Jesus, the Christ, I pray. Amen*

Chapter 5

Becoming a True Worshipper: Fulfilling God's Creative Purpose

As John 4:23 says, it's time, as worshipers of God, to give him all we have. For when he is exalted, everything about me is decreased. So many times we stand in the way of really stepping into the secret place of worship with God. Just abandon tradition and the "expected" ways of Praise & Worship and get lost in the holy of holies with the sole intention of blessing the Father's heart. ~ Jessica Leah Springer

Worship means different things to different people. Unfortunately, there is not a clear definition of *worship* in the Scriptures. There is not a specific word for worship that is used across the board.

There also are many ways to express worship. Some say that we worship God by singing songs and spiritual hymns. Some say that it is the lifting of hands and the bowing down and laying prostrate in God's presence. Some say it is praising and thanking God. And, others say worship only occurs in certain locations, such as in a church building.

There once was a woman at a well in Samaria, who was confused about worship, in part because of an ongoing argument between Jews and Samaritans over where people should worship. This woman entered into a discussion with Jesus, and Jesus helped her realize what is at the heart of worship:

> [T]he hour is coming when you will neither on this mountain, nor in Jerusalem, worship the Father. ***But the hour is coming, and now is, when the true worshipers will worship the Father in spirit and truth; for the Father is seeking such to worship Him. God is Spirit, and those who worship Him must worship in spirit and truth. (John 4:21-24)

Jesus was speaking prophetically about a future time when the Holy Spirit would indwell each believer. Well, that time is now. Through Jesus Christ, each of us has been indwelt with the Holy Spirit. We have been given the greatest gift of all, the Holy Spirit, and we now have the capacity and privilege to worship God in spirit and truth. God has given us Himself, through Jesus Christ and in the person of the Holy Spirit. He is the one who lives in us to enable us to offer authentic worship to the God of our salvation.

As many of you, for years I thought worship simply was a Sunday morning service experience. Each Sunday, we would go to our local church to hear the pastor's sermon and the choir's songs. *Worship* was my family's Sunday religious activity, and it was very important to us. I enjoyed the church service, but more often than not, I returned home continuing life as usual; there was no dramatic change in the way that I lived. My knowledge of worship was limited and mostly associated with what happened at church.

It wasn't until my mid 20's that my perception of worship was to change forever. I was invited to a Sunday night worship service at a church in Los Angeles. The praise team and choir were singing what they called *praise and worship songs.* I had never heard or sung songs that were in adoration and exaltation of the Father and Jesus. But, most of the song lyrics came from Scripture, and I soon began to sing along. As I sang, I felt exhilarated and overjoyed. It was as if my body and emotions could not contain themselves. My eyes filled with tears and, before I knew it, my hands were lifted up, my knees became weak, and I hit the floor. The Spirit of God began to move within me, and I found myself exalting and praising – yes, *worshipping* Jesus. There was no concern for how foolish I looked. In fact, I didn't see anyone around me. It was just Jesus and me. His presence engulfed me like flames of fire. I felt only His love surrounding and flowing from Him to me.

It was more than just an experience, though. From that day forward, the way I lived radically changed. I began to understand that worship is more than a song or sermon, but it is about God and who He is. For the first time, I realized that God is the source, subject, and focus of worship.

Worship is all about God. God created worship and created us to worship Him. Worship begins and ends with Him and not us. The Holy Spirit has been given to every believer so that we can worship God in spirit and in truth (John 4:23 & 14:17). None of us can become true worshippers without Him. It really doesn't matter *where* we worship God; the key is *that* we worship God. Although singing songs of praise are part of the worship experience, it is not exclusive, for true worship is about a lifestyle of honoring, revering, serving, and adoring God. Every area of our lives should reflect our worship of God. God desires that we offer ourselves to Him in worship. The Apostle Paul tells us that, in view of God's mercy, we are to offer our bodies as living sacrifices, holy and pleasing to God – this is our true and proper worship (Romans 12:1-2). God not only wants us to worship Him through psalms and hymns and spiritual songs (Ephesians 5:19) as well as through praise and thanksgiving, but God desires us to surrender our bodies, wills, and our very lives to Him. Everything that we do, whatever we eat or drink, we do to the glory of God (1 Corinthians 10:31). This is the life of worship that He delights in. Words alone, no matter how lovely, cannot satisfy God. It is our lives, in submission to His will and in spiritual service, that He desires. Only when our lives are poured out to Him as an offering, can real transformation take place. And, that's when we become true worshippers, when we not only undergo an *exchange* but a *change*. The natural is exchanged for the spiritual and the heavenly, and we are changed from glory to glory and become more like Christ.

When I think of worship, there is no one in the Bible who embodied worship like King David. David did not have the indwelt Holy Spirit as we do. But, we are told that the Spirit of the Lord came upon Him (1 Samuel 16:13) and allowed this man to worship God in ways like none other. David loved the Lord with all his heart, soul, and strength, and He commanded every fiber of His body to bless the Lord. In Psalm 103:1, David vows to, "[b]less the Lord, O my soul; [a]nd all that is within me, bless His holy name." David was an unrestrained worshipper. He literally danced in the streets, nearly naked, but not ashamed of worshipping the God who had been so good and merciful to him. God wrote worship on the heart of David, and David revered, exalted, and esteemed the Lord. Throughout the Psalms, we can see David's heart of worship. Worship was not only a part of his life; it was how he lived his life.

There is one Psalm in particular that comes to mind and provides great insight into the heart of David, the worshipper of God. Psalm 63 begins, "O God, You are my God; early will I seek You; my soul thirsts for You; my body longs for You in a dry and weary land where there is no water." That psalm finishes with "[b]ut the king will rejoice in God; all who swear by God's name will praise him, while the mouths of liars will be silenced." David longed for God's presence with every inch of his being. Even when He had sinned against God, he recognized that he could not live without the presence of God in his life (Psalm51).

David not only revered, adored, honored, respected, and extolled God openly and vocally, he also worshipped God privately. In Psalm 63:6-7, David shared that on his bed he remembered God. He thought of Him through the night watches. Because God was his help, he rejoiced in the shadow of His wings. From this, we learn that David had submitted even His thoughts to the worship of God. Even at night, he meditated on goodness of the God. He truly worshipped God with all His heart.

According to Judson Cornwall, "[w]orship is written upon the heart of man by the hand of God.... In a broad sense, worship is inseparable from God. You cannot have an intimate relationship with God unless you enter into this life of worship." Similarly, singer and author Darlene Zschech comments that, "[a]s a true worshipper, your heart will long to worship Him at all times, in all ways, and with all your life."

We have been given an eternal invitation to become God's instruments of worship. Our worship is the highest calling and expression of our love for our Father. Although one form of worship involves bowing down and laying prostrate before the Lord, perhaps the most acceptable worship is demonstrated by a heart that bows down to the control and will of our Father. I believe that is what God finds pleasure in.

Our Father wants us to choose to worship Him. If we choose not to worship Him, we miss one of the greatest opportunities for intimacy and fellowship with our Lord. And, if we fail to worship Him now, one day we will; the time is coming when every knee will bow and every tongue will confess Christ as Lord (Philippians 2:10-11).

When we choose to focus our affection and devotion towards God and to surrender our hearts and wills to Him, something incredible happens. Our lives are brought into order and in line with God's will for us; bondages are broken; and peace and joy fill our hearts. As true worshippers, we recognize His worth, glorious majesty, supremacy, and authority. As we give our best and all to our Lord, He gives us so much more; He gives us Himself.

And, by engaging in worship, we join the angels and all creation in declaring God's glory. In the book of Revelation, John said that he saw and heard the voice of many angels, living creatures, and elders, numbering ten thousand times ten thousand, crying out in a loud voice: "Worthy is the Lamb, who was slain, to receive power and wealth and wisdom and strength and honor and glory and praise!" (Rev 5:11-12) Only the Lord is worthy of all praise and worship.

I challenge you, today, to open your heart to worship. Allow worship to flow from the depth of your heart and show itself in the very way you live your life. Don't be comfortable with just your usual Sunday worship experience; stretch yourself to experience God's presence in your daily life. Offer and surrender your body and mind to God's control, and focus on pleasing Him. Release the worshipper – the Holy Spirit – within you so that He can give voice to your worship and so that all you do and say magnifies and glorifies God. You will be surprised at the response of God, the Father. He will shower you with His love and presence, and you will experience a little bit of heaven on earth.

> *Lord,*
>
> For years, I thought that I knew how to worship you, only to discover that I knew so little about true worship. Lord, teach me to worship. You are the author, the beginning, and the ending of worship. No man can teach me like you. I want to worship you with my heart, soul and mind. Teach me how to do this. I promise I will submit and surrender my life to you. Help me to focus on you and your goodness. Only by your Spirit can I be the true worshipper who worships in spirit and in truth. Teach me, Lord. I want to know how to worship you.
>
> It's in the Name of Jesus. Amen

Chapter 6

The Abundant Life: Obedience and Victory over Sin

Most of us labor under the delusion that we have every right to our lives; that we have the right to go where we wish, do as we please, live as we choose, and decide our own destiny. We do not. We belong to God. He made us for himself. He chose us in Christ out of love, from before the foundation of the earth to be his own. He has bought us twice over, both through his generous death and also by his amazing resurrection life. ~Phillip Keller

No matter how much we say we love the Lord, there is still that old nature that wants ultimate power and control. Somehow, we think that we know what to do with our lives and how to handle on our destinies. We want to control our lives and futures.

If you are anything like me, you may have struggled at times with the decision whether to obey God or to do as you please. Early in my Christian walk, this was a constant challenge, and I failed in obedience miserably. It wasn't that I wanted to be disobedient; I was just so accustomed to doing things my own way and being in control of my life. When I began to grow in the knowledge of God and the word, I really worked hard at trying to obey God and to be righteous. I thought that, if I tried and worked hard, my prayers would be answered. In reality, the more I tried to obey God and become righteous, the more difficult it was to do. I found myself going two steps forward and four steps backward. No matter how purposeful I was in my efforts, obedience could not be accomplished on my own.

The Apostle Paul experienced this challenge as well.

I want to do what is good, but I don't. I don't want to do what is wrong, but I do it anyway. But if I do what I don't want to do, I am not really the one doing wrong; it is sin living in me that does it. I have discovered this principle of life – that when I want to do what is right, I inevitably do what is wrong. I love God's law with all my heart. But there is another power within me that is at war with my mind. This power makes me a slave to the sin that is still within me. Oh, what a miserable person I am! Who will free me from this life that is dominated by sin and death? Thank God! The answer is in Jesus Christ our Lord. So you see how it is: In my mind I really want to obey God's law, but because of my sinful nature I am a slave to sin." (Romans 7:17-25 Message)

It is simply crazy to think that we know more about our lives and what is best for us than our Creator. God is the only one incomparable and omniscient, able to tell us our future and our ending, and capable of assuring us that He will be with us for the long haul (Isaiah 46:10). He is also the only one that we can depend upon to show up and take care of us. I like what the Message Bible has to say about our efforts at achieving obedience out of our own perceived sufficiency.

> *Let me put this question to you: How did your new life begin? Was it by working your heads off to please God? Or was it by responding to God's message to you? Are you going to continue this craziness? For only crazy people would think they could complete by their own efforts what was begun by God. If you weren't smart enough or strong enough to begin it how do you suppose you could perfect it?* (Galatians 3:2-3)

There is no way that we can obey God outside of Christ. We all have been born in sin and iniquity, and only through the power of Christ and the Holy Spirit can anything we do be acceptable and righteous before God (Roman 6:4).

There are daily deterrents that keep us from obeying and pleasing God. We live in a fallen world, and we are constantly in spiritual warfare whether we realize it or not. However, we have a perfect example in Jesus, who was tempted in the same ways we are, yet He was able to endure those temptations without sin (Hebrews 4:15). Because of what He experienced, Christ is sympathetic with our human condition. He understands our temptation and propensity to sin. Though surrounded by the corruption of this world, He did not fall or sin; He humbled Himself, surrendering His will to the will of the Father to redeem our lives from destruction (Philippians 2:8). In surrendering His will, Jesus gave ear to what the Father commanded, executed His command, submitted to the Father's will and authority, and yielded every impulse and emotion to what was set before Him. Christ is our ultimate example of obedience, setting the standard and paving the way for our righteousness and victory over sin. He always did what the Father commanded Him to do. He lived to please the Father.

Every believer has been given the power to be obedient and to withstand temptation in the same way, through Christ and the power of the Holy Spirit who indwells us. Jesus said that we cannot call Him Lord, if we do not do what He says (Luke 6:46). Although we can't do it on our own, we can depend on the Holy Spirit to lead us to nothing less than a life that models Christ. It is not a life of doing what we please but a life of finding out what He requires of us and then doing that. Obedience is simply doing exactly what God instructs us to do because we love and honor Him as the supreme authority in our lives.

Jesus said that, if we love Him, we will keep His commandments (John 14:15). Jesus also told His disciples that He had loved them as the Father loved Him, and He asked them to make themselves at home in His love. He promised that, if they kept God's commands, they would remain intimately in His love (John 15:9-10). The promise and the expectation is the same for us. If we do not obey God words or commands, we are liars, and the truth is not in us. On the other hand, if we do obey His word, God's love is made complete in us (1 John 2:3-5), and we are at home in His love. There is no way that we can separate love from obedience. They are intricately connected. Our love is expressed to God by our obedience, because obedience fulfills God's command to love. It is impossible to love and know God without obeying Him. No sacrificial offering is as acceptable as obeying God and His word (1 Samuel 15:22).

Imagine, though, how great the challenge would be, if we were called to be obedient without instruction about what is required of us. Without adequate knowledge and understanding of God's word, we will not know what God expects of us. Neither will we know His provisions for us. Obedience is tied to being in the word of God and having the word of God in you.

There is no better life to live than one of obedience, but it is a matter of choice. Love means doing what God has commanded. The real test of love is obeying God and His word. Obedience to God's commands is the sure test of love. The choice is ours – obedience and blessings or disobedience and consequences.

We can choose life or death, blessings or curses (Deuteronomy 30:19). If we choose obedience and life, Scripture promises that we can experience an abundant life full of blessings and favor (Deuteronomy 30:15-16). However, if we choose disobedience and death, we are rebelling against the authority and wisdom of God and can expect destruction and confusion.

What God requires of us is not burdensome. Obedience yields great dividends. If we are obedient, God promises to bless us in our cities and countries, our children and those in our wombs, our land, our workplaces, our houses, and the work of our hands. He will provide rain on the ground in the right season. He will make us lenders and not borrowers, the head and not the tail, and above and not on the bottom (Deuteronomy 28: 1-12).

These promises and blessing are ours. We can have victory over sin. We can succeed because Jesus put sin to death on the cross. The old life has died, and the new life now is hidden with God in Christ (Colossians

3:3). We have victory over sin because of Christ. We are the children of God by faith in Jesus Christ, and we are one in Christ. We are Abraham's seed and heirs according to the promise (Galatians 3:26-29). When we are willing and obedient, God will give us His best. He will even cause us to feast like Kings (Isaiah 1:19). He will throw us a lavish party and serve us His good stuff, filled with His blessings and love.

Dear Father,

It is my desire to please you. At times I seem to fail you, not because I want to, but a struggle exists within me between doing what is right and what is wrong. Lord, I cannot do this alone. Thank you for the Holy Spirit, my Helper. When I am weak, He makes me strong. When I need conviction and convincing, He confronts me. Thank you I never have to do this on my own. He stands by me. I acknowledge the grace that has been given me through Jesus Christ. I thank him for paying the price for my sins and mistakes past, present, and future. You see me through the lens of His righteousness and declare me righteous. Thank you for Jesus. It is in His Name to Jesus. Amen

Chapter 7

Welcome Holy Spirit: My Friend, Advocate, and Revealer of Truth

Wise leaders should have known that the human heart cannot exist in a vacuum. If Christians are forbidden to enjoy the wine of the Spirit they will turn to the wine of the flesh.... Christ died for our hearts and the Holy Spirit wants to come and satisfy them. ~A. W. Tozer

Is something missing in your life, even though you are a Christian? Are you lacking power? Lacking peace? Having trouble keeping love and joy in your life? Well, it could be that you have overlooked one of the greatest gifts that the Christian has been given – the power of the Holy Spirit.

For years, that was my experience, and it also has been the experience of some of our greatest Christian leaders. One day, I was visiting one of our associate pastors. This pastor is a connoisseur of Christian books and literature. He and I had just begun a study on the Holy Spirit, and I was looking for more resources on the subject. Although I knew quite a bit about the ministry of the Holy Spirit, I felt that I could still learn more. While looking through his library, I found a book on the life of D.L. Moody, written by Paul Davis, called "Holy Ghost and Fire." I had been interested in the life of D.L. Moody, especially given that I attended Moody Bible Institute for a short time and knew a number of the school's graduates. So, this seemed a perfect book to add to my reading list.

In reading the book, I discovered that D.L. Moody ended up as a man full of the Holy Spirit. His ministry did not begin that way, however. For years, he preached the gospel, delivering harsh sermons that focused on hell and damnation, but something was missing. Then, one day he met two ladies, who were prayer warriors. They shared with Moody that, although he had received salvation, he lacked the power of the Holy Spirit in his life. So, they committed that, as he preached, they would pray for him to be baptized with the Holy Spirit and fire. And, that they did.

Supported by their prayers, a hunger began to well up in Moody's soul for the baptism of the Holy Spirit. Moody said that he didn't know what it was, but he began to cry out as never before. He reached the point where he decided that he would rather die than not have the Spirit's power. The problem was that, despite his hunger, the power would not come. He experienced such agony that he rolled on the floor, flooded with tears and crying to God to be baptized with the Holy Ghost. What he didn't realize was that God was not fulfilling his request because he had refused to do what God had asked of him. It wasn't until Moody came to the end of himself, and surrendered his will to the will of God, that the last chain snapped. Immediately an overpowering sense of God's presence flooded his soul. The Spirit of the Almighty God had come to him.

Without wasting a moment's time, Moody locked himself in a nearby friend's room so he could be alone with God. The room seemed ablaze with God. He stretched out on the floor and lay bathing his soul in the Divine. Of this communion and mountain top experience Moody later wrote, "I can only say that God revealed Himself to me, and I had such an experience of His love that I had to ask Him to stay His hand." From that day until his death, God remolded and gave him a gentle and sweet spirit. He submitted his life to the management of the Holy Spirit. What a sweet surrender! According to Moody, "I was all the time tugging and carrying the water but now I have a river that carries me." (John 7:37-39)

Reading about Moody's journey prompted me to recall my first experience with the Holy Spirit. As a teenager and young adult, I knew very little about the Holy Spirit and who He is. I thought that He was an "it" or some type of force. I did not know that that He is as much God as both the Father and the Son are. He simply functions in a different capacity.

I remember when my perspective of the Holy Spirit changed. A friend invited me to see Kathryn Kulman, a well-known evangelist who was recognized for the miracles that took place under her ministry. She often came to the Shrine Auditorium in Los Angeles, and I also had seen her several times on TV. There was something about this woman that mesmerized me. She was such a gentle and delicate looking woman. When she walked, it was as if she was gliding on air; it was somewhat angelic. She would come out on stage singing songs, and then she would raise her hands and invite the presence of the Holy Spirit. She seemed to yield completely to His control. As she welcomed the presence of the Holy Spirit, He would fill the place, and there would be hundreds of salvations, healings, other miracles, and the word of knowledge and prophecy. I can truly say that we experienced the presence of God; it was though we were being treated to a glimpse of heaven while on earth.

It took only one experience, seeing the power of the Holy Spirit, to transform my life. I began to hunger for this wonderful experience more and more. I wanted the Holy Spirit to show up in my life that way. I wanted to know Him as my friend and companion as she did. Shortly after this experience, I rededicated my life to Christ. I asked for the infilling of the Holy Spirit, and He flooded my life with His presence and power, and I have never been the same.

A wonderful part of this new life has been learning about and experiencing the Holy Spirit's ministry. He has been my steady companion, even though there have been times that I have not honored His presence or acknowledge Him. Thankfully, He has never left me alone and each time has remained at my side waiting to renew our relationship. You see, the Holy Spirit will never force His will or Himself on us. He waits patiently for us to invite Him to be our power source, friend, companion, and advocate. When we do, He continues His work in us. I dare not do anything in this life without relying on Him to anoint, lead, and guide me. I am like a dancer every day, waiting for Him to lead me to the next step. I know that, with Him as my partner, teacher, and counsel, I will always have a successful ending.

The Holy Spirit is not a force or mystical entity, as I thought for many years. Instead, He is the personification of the power of God. He is God, the third person of the Trinity, and He represents the Triune God. He is eternal, not having a beginning or an ending (Hebrew 9:14). He is omnipotent, having all power (Luke 1:35). He is omnipresent, being everywhere (Psalm 139:7). He is omniscient, understanding all things (1 Corinthians

2:10, 11). He is divine. The Holy Spirit can be grieved (Ephesians 4:30). He intercedes for us (Romans 8:26-27) and distributes spiritual gifts to us according to His will (1 Corinthians 12:7-11). He is the personal representative of the Godhead on earth. He is the believer's superintendent and the administrator of the Church of Jesus Christ. He is our personal connection with the Spirit of God and acts as God's interpreter and revealer of truth in our lives.

The same reverence that we give the Father and Jesus should be given to the person of the Holy Spirit. If God the Father and the Son acknowledged the necessity of the Holy Spirit in the creation and of His seed to bring about the incarnate Christ, and if Jesus needed His anointing for His ministry on earth, then we certainly need His power to live like Christ. Jesus did not do anything apart from the Holy Spirit's involvement. As Jesus readied the disciples for His departure, He asked the Father to send the Holy Spirit to teach and guide them in all truth, to be their friend and advocate, and to empower them to do the work that was ahead (John 14:16).

The good news is that the same Holy Spirit, who was sent for the early believers and who abides in me, also dwells in you. Every believer is indwelt by the Holy Spirit. We are His temples; He lives in us. He is never far away.

The Holy Spirit desires to be our friend and daily companion. We can talk to Him, and He will speak. We can tell Him our thoughts, challenges, and our heart's desires. When we need spiritual insight or understanding of the word of God, He is our teacher and the interpreter of God's truths. He will be that inward witness that will nudge us when we begin to stray from the truth. He will never leave us or forsake us, and we can depend on Him to be our standby, enabler, and lawyer when there is a need. He will constantly remind us of what Christ has done for us and how much He loves us. Do we not want this precious gift? Do we not want to be continually filled with His presence (Ephesians 1:8)? If we answer, "Yes," He will continually fill us with His divine presence and do exceedingly abundantly above anything we can think of or ask (Ephesians 3:20). We do not have to struggle or even beg to be filled. All we need to do is ask our Father and then receive this extravagant gift.

Dear Father,

Fill me continually with your Holy Spirit and refresh me with your presence. I want to experience you fully so that out my belly rivers of living water will flow causing someone to know Christ. May there be an overflowing of love and mercy and a demonstration of your power and glory in my life so that others will know that you are my Father. Help me to hear your voice and discern your movement in my life.

In Jesus' Name, I pray. Amen

Chapter 8

Loving the Way God Loves

If you took the love of all the best mothers and fathers who ever lived (think about that for a moment)—all the goodness, kindness, patience, fidelity, wisdom, tenderness, strength and love—and united all those virtues in one person, that person would only be a faint shadow of the love and mercy in the heart of God for you and me.
-Brennan Manning

> *What the world needs now is love, sweet love. It's the only thing that there's just too little of. What the world needs now is love, sweet love, no, not just for some but for everyone.*
>
> *Lord, we don't need another mountain. There are mountains and hillsides enough to climb. There are oceans and rivers enough to cross, enough to last till the end of time. What the world needs now is love, sweet love. It's the only thing that there's just too little of. What the world needs now is love, sweet love, no, not just for some but for everyone.*

Lord, we don't need another meadow. There are cornfields and wheat fields enough to grow. There are sunbeams and moonbeams enough to shine, oh listen, Lord, if you want to know. What the world needs now is love, sweet love. It's the only thing that there's just too little of. What the world needs now is love, sweet love, no, not just for some but for everyone. ~Burt Bacharach and Hal David

I used to hear that song when I was a young teenager. I remember singing and humming it; the song resonated in my mind over and over again.

Everyone needs love. If we are honest, we will admit that we all are looking for love now, or we have been at various points in our lives. And, if we continue our honesty, we'll acknowledge that sometimes we looked for that love in the wrong places and from the wrong people.

Fundamentally, as humans, we have this need for someone to care for and value us affectionately. Likewise, we want someone to whom we can show affection or endear. We associate these desires with what we call *love*. But, *love* is an interesting word. We use the same word to describe the clothes we wear, the food we eat, the television programs we prefer, the preachers we favor, the people and pets in our lives, and the list could go on. Considering the range of applications, it's probably an understatement to conclude that the word *love* has been loosely used, misinterpreted, and misunderstood.

You see, we define *love* based on our human reasoning and our experiences, but God has a different perspective. God is love, and He created love.

From the beginning, the word *love* has been connected to God. God has always desired a covenant love relationship with His people. He called them the apple of His eyes, a peculiar and special people to Him. He was passionately and affectionately in love with His people in the Old Testament, and He is just as much in love with us, the seed of Abraham. We know that because He allowed Christ's blood to be shed to redeem us through the covenant of grace. All love originated with God and is born of God. It doesn't matter whether it is Agape (God's unconditional love), Eros (passionate love), Philia (brotherly love), or Storge (affection); they all flow from the love of God. All are expressions of God's love.

For years I could not make the distinction between them. I didn't know much about God's love, the Agape kind of love. I had experienced both the Eros and the Philia love. I had many friends with whom I shared Philia love and a few with whom I had been romantically involved or the Eros love. However, for years I didn't know that Agape even existed; I simply did not know God and could not see or touch Him. I knew of God's love only vicariously, only through what I was told.

I remember my first experience with what I called *love*, what I learned later to be Eros love. I was about 14 years old, when I met this young man who was attracted to me; it was mutual. My thoughts were consumed with him to the point that I was unable to concentrate on my studies. I would write his name next to mine and draw a small heart through our names. Every thought of him would cause my heart to pulsate. When he held my hand, I got weak in the knees and sweaty palms. He was the object of my affection...for a time, anyway. In less than a year that relationship ended. Those feelings didn't last, and thank God, neither did the relationship.

Over the years, there were other relationships that I mistook for love. Some were good and others were hurtful, painful, and disappointing. Each experience shaped my perspective on love, and some even left me with a jaded view. As those relationships fizzled or failed, my faith in love dissipated, and I became very cautious about relationships.

Though painful, my experiences with Eros love were not wasted. These early relationship failures were for my good in the end. I recognized that, as humans, we will fail each other because that is our nature. However, as I wandered for years, searching for answers regarding my own failed relationships, I actually found myself seeking God. In searching for answers, I discovered the arms of God. He was waiting to introduce me to a loving, intimate, personal, and trusting relationship...with Him. My eyes began to open, and I realized and understood for the first time that God's love is different than the sappy, romantic, and sometimes flawed love that I had experienced. God's love is absolute goodness. It is unfailing and everlasting. And, God promises us, just as He did Joshua, that He will always be with us and never fail us (Joshua 1:5). God's love never fails (Psalm 136).

Human love can't compare to God's love. God's love is beyond human understanding. The human mind can't understand the depth, breadth, and height of God's love (Ephesians 3:18). God's nature is love, and He expresses who He is through His love. Scripture states that this is how God showed His love among us; He sent His one and only Son into the world that we might live through Him (John 3:16). This is love: not that we loved God, but that He loved us and sent His Son as an atoning sacrifice for our sins. Since God so loved us, we also ought to love one another (1 John 4:9-10). Our mere existence is evidence of God's love for us. He doesn't just love; He is love. Everything that flows from Him, to and for us, stems from His love. Nothing can ever separate us from His love. The Apostle Paul wrote:

For I am convinced that neither death nor life, neither angels nor demons, neither the present nor the future, nor any powers, neither height nor depth, nor anything else in all creation, will be able to separate us from the love of God that is in Christ Jesus our Lord. (Romans 8:38-39)

We will never be able to escape the love of God. No matter where we are, His love will find us. There is absolutely nothing that will keep Him from passionately pursuing a love relationship with us. His love is for us all – saint or sinner. It is not short-lived, nor will it fade away. It is constant and ever flowing from Him, and it is now flowing through us to others.

God has deposited His love in each believer through the indwelt Holy Spirit. The Holy Spirit transmits God's love to every fiber of our being. Because God's love resides in us, we then have the capacity to be conduits, dispensers, and vessels of His love. When His love flows through us to others, then Christ is personified in our lives. The world recognizes that we come from Him and that we are His disciples (John 13:34-35). As we live in God's love, we live in God and God in us. If we are unable to love those that we see, how can we love our God whom we have not seen (1 John 4:14-20)?

It is not enough just to talk about love; we are called to be conduits of God's love. Jesus was asked, "Teacher, which is the greatest commandment in the law?" He replied, "'You shall love the Lord your God with all your heart, and with all your soul, and with your entire mind.' This is the great and foremost commandment, and there is a second like it: 'You shall love your neighbors as yourself.' The whole Law and Prophets hang on these two commands." (Matthew 22:37-40; Mark 12:28-34)

There is no other law that is as great as the law of love. We may speak words with power, revealing mysteries. We may have faith to move mountains. But, if we do not have and practice God's love, we are nothing. Even if we give everything we own to the poor or die a martyr, if we do not have love, we are bankrupt (1 Corinthians 13). Nothing can substitute for the love of God and His love that indwells us.

God's love is at work in every believer. All we need to do is yield to it and submit to the Holy Spirit, who is at work to perform exceedingly and abundantly in and through us to benefit those whom God loves. As children of God, we have a fiduciary responsibility to be the arms and hands of love in a lost and hurting world. We can demonstrate His love by loving the way He loves. God's love is patient. It is benevolent. It is not jealous. It does not parade itself. It does not puff itself up. It is not rude. It does not seek its own. It is not sharpened. It does not calculate evil. It does not find joy in unrighteousness, but it enjoys the truth. It protectively covers all things. It believes all things. It hopes all things. It patiently endures all things. God's love never fails (1 Corinthians 13).

Father,

I desire to love others and myself as you have loved me. Please show me how to walk out this life of love as Christ did. Show me how to be kind, tender-hearted, patient, and forgiving. I submit my will and emotions to the Holy Spirit who abides in me. May the Spirit of Christ dwell in my heart so that I will be rooted and grounded in your love? Help me to understand the breadth, and length, and depth, and height of your love, and to know the love and peace of Christ, which surpasses my knowledge, so that I may be filled with all the fullness of God.

In the Name of your Son, Jesus the Christ, I pray. Amen

Chapter 9

Living for His Glory

"God created us for this: to live our lives in a way that makes him look more like the greatness and the beauty and the infinite worth that he really is. This is what it means to be created in the image of God."
— <u>John Piper</u>

Throughout the book we have discussed some of the foundational truths and practices that are needed if our lives are to glorify God. The discussion has included the importance of knowing the God of our creation and pursuing an intimate relationship with Him, communing and fellowshipping with Him in prayer, discovering who we are in God's word, practicing a lifestyle of worship, living victoriously over sin, embracing the guidance of the Holy Spirit, and loving like God loves. These truths have been essential to my spiritual growth and development and have been crucial to sustaining an intimate relationship with my Lord. It has been my delight to share with you these truths and the experiences with the Father whom I hold so dear.

Choosing to live for God's glory is the greatest honor that we can give Him. It is our humble response to a Father who has been so good to us. It is our dearest offering to the God who loved us so much that He made us in His image and likeness so we could mirror His goodness, holiness, wisdom, mercy, splendor, love, power, and presence in the world. It is what we render to God, who is pure, loving, and good and who has chosen us to be the light of the world and salt of earth through His Son, Jesus Christ.

If never before, today, the world needs to experience the glory of God. Without a doubt, the world is in turmoil – economic upheavals, political and civil unrest, sexual immorality, wars and rumors of wars, not to mention earthquakes and all sorts of environmental and ecological changes and disasters. Our children are being enticed, and some taken captive, by unprecedented evil bombarding them through peers, who are confused and lack moral guidance, and through a range of cyber temptations. People all over the world are searching for answers.

Would you be surprised if I told you that *you* have the answer to the world's problems? His Name is Jesus. He has been made wisdom unto us from God (1 Corinthians 2:16) and His Spirit lives in us. Because we are in Christ, we have the mind of Christ – the thoughts, intent, and purposes of His heart. In Jesus is the spirit of wisdom, understanding, counsel, and might (Isaiah 11:2). We are His ambassadors, representatives, and emissaries. On earth, we are the highest ranking officials authorized to speak on His behalf, and we are to show forth His glory, wisdom, power, and might. We are the vessels, the carriers, of His manifest glory. So, if this is so, why doesn't the world seek us out?

The answer is simple, but not pleasant. We have hid our light under a bushel and faded into the world's darkness. There is little that distinguishes us from others. We have taken on so much of the world's habits and character that sometimes we bear little resemblance to Christ. We do not manifest His presence or make Him recognizable in us because we don't acknowledge that His Spirit is alive in us. Often, we ignore the fact that the Holy Spirit has taken residence in us and that we are His temple.

However, we have all that is necessary to light this world with His glory. We have been empowered by God Himself. As Christ was the light of God's glory, we have the capacity to be the light of Christ's glory (**2 Corinthians 4:6).** Jesus told us:

You are the salt of the earth; but if the salt has lost its taste, how shall its saltiness be restored? *** You are the light of the world. A city set on a hill cannot be hid. *** Let your light so shine before men, that they may see your good works and give glory to your Father who is in heaven. (Matthew 5:13-16)

If the world is to see the glory of God or if the glory of God is to be revealed, until Jesus returns it has to be revealed through us. In order for that to happen, though, we must cooperate with the Holy Spirit and allow Him to transform our lives into the image of Christ. However, He is a gentleman and will never force His will over ours. We must be willing to work with Him, to surrender and submit our lives and our wills to His control. Jesus is our example. Jesus was the expressed image of the Father on earth, possessing His fullness, His character, His attributes, and the light of His glory. Just as Jesus reflected the Father, we can become the expressed image of Jesus. The world is waiting to see the real Jesus and His character from those who claim Him as Messiah. If the people of the world are to know Jesus, guess what? We are it! People should see the invisible Jesus in the very visible us. When asked about our Savior, wouldn't it be wonderful if we could confidently respond that, when you see me, you see Christ.

When Phillip asked Jesus to show him the Father, Jesus pointed to Himself.

Don't you know me, Philip, even after I have been among you such a long time? Anyone who has seen me has seen the Father. How can you say, 'Show us the Father'? Don't you believe that I am in the Father, and that the Father is in me? The words I say to you I do not speak on my own authority. Rather, it is the Father, living in me, who is doing his work. Believe me when I say that I am in the Father and the Father is in me; or at least believe on the evidence of the works themselves. (John 14:9-11)

Christ was honored to say that He was of God. Everything that He did on earth glorified God. Well, Christ, the hope of glory, is in us. His glory and anointing abides in us. Christ spoke with His Father's authority because it had been given Him (John 17:1-5). As He was one with the Father, we are now one with Him. We have been given authority through Christ to speak on behalf of the Father and the Son. Jesus prayed that we would be one with the Father, and so we are. Christ has given us His authority and glory (John17:20-23). This is our time and season to bear His glory and authority, to give His wisdom to the world, and to share the good news of the gospel. It is time for us to *be* the gospel – living epistles read by men. We have the solution. The world is waiting for us. Will you represent? Will you live for His glory in the world?

If you choose to accept His invitation to live for His glory, to display His goodness, love, holiness, splendor, majesty, beauty, compassion and wisdom, He will not only endue you with power but manifest His Shekinah presence. His Shekinah glory will show up, and there will be times when you will see and feel the weighted presence of God in your midst. God wants to show up in your life so that others will know that He has sent you and that the Spirit of Christ lives in you. He has anointed you with the Holy Spirit to do good and to heal as He did with Jesus. Scripture tells us that God anointed Jesus with the Holy Spirit and power, and He went around doing good and healing many who were under the power of the devil, because God was with Him. Today, God wants to manifest Himself to the world through us. Will you determine that you will live for no other purpose than for His glory?

We have been charged with the responsibility of living the message of the good news and shining so brightly that those who are in darkness will be drawn to the light of God's glory. I have to admit, lest you think I have arrived or I am perfect, that I have not fully lived my life for God's glory and exemplified the spirit and character of Christ in all my doings. However, I am determined that I will get there. God has been gracious to me, and He is gracious to all of us. He continues to manifest His presence, glory, and power in my life. I now sing this song and hope that one day it will be my reality. "To the glory of God I give my heart; to the glory of God I give my soul; to the glory of God I give my life; I give all and all to glory of God."

I thank God for the amazing generosity of His grace and mercy towards me. He continues to show up in me and through me as I strive to live for His glory. It is my prayer that you will join me on this journey of living for His glory and accept this extravagant invitation to bear His fruit; goodness, holiness, majesty, mercy, beauty, splendor, love, and miraculous power in the world. Let others get a glimpse of His glory, which abides in His Son Jesus and now is in us because we are in Christ. Yes, we have been *Made in His Image to Live for His Glory!*

Lord,

I have no other desire than to live a life that pleases you. I want to show forth your glory, goodness, mercy, splendor, love, and majesty to those who are without the light of your glory. Lord, help me to reflect who you are in the world through Christ. Let your presence be manifested in my life so that others may be saved, healed, and delivered. Give me the wisdom that comes from you to have an answer for everyone who asks of the hope that is within me. Help me to point them to my Savior, Jesus the Christ. Help me to live for your glory.

In the Name of Jesus, the Messiah, the Anointed One, Full of God's glory, Amen.

Living for God's Glory

Living for His Glory is what I have been called to
Exemplifying His goodness in all that I say and do
Living for His glory to make the world aware
That in us, Jesus' Spirit is alive and his presence is everywhere
Living for His glory spreading the gospel of love
Proclaiming salvation that comes from Christ, the Father's beloved
Living for His glory that is the only thing that satisfies
No other thing can substitute for it is His spirit in us that abides
Living for His glory letting His light shine
Giving hope to those in darkness and giving sight to the blind
Living for His glory is the ultimate honor to give
To someone who sent His Son to die so that we could live
Living for His glory
What a life to live!
Living for His glory there is no other life for me
Being a Reflector of His glory that's what we have been called to be
Pleasing our Father and living for His Glory
I invite you to join me!

Jocelyn Whitfield

Introduction

Isaiah 47:3

Hebrews 1:3

Chapter 1

The Extravagant Generosity of God's Grace: Knowing God Personally and Intimately

John 17:3

Jeremiah 9:23, 24

1Samuael

Genesis 1:1

Genesis 2:4

Genesis 15: 2

Genesis 17:1, 2

Genesis 22:1-19

Exodus 17:15

Exodus 15:22-27

Chapter 2
The Gift of Prayer: Communing and Fellowshipping with Our Heavenly Father

Matthew 6:9-13

Romans 8:26

1Samuel 30:7-8

2Timothy 1:7

Hebrew 4:12

Romans 10:17

Isaiah 55:11

Jeremiah 1:12

Mark 16-17-18

John 14:14

John 14:13

John 16:23

Philippians 2; 9

Acts 4:12 & 10:43

1John 2:12

Philippians 2:10

Hebrews 4:16

Chapter 3
Finding the Real Life in God's Word

Isaiah 44:24-26

Matthews 4:4

Hebrews 4:12

Psalm 1:2-3

Joshua 1:8

2nd Timothy 3:16, 17

2nd Corinthians 3:2-3

Chapter 4
Embracing the God Kind of Life: Walking by Faith

Romans 12:3

Hebrews 11:6

Hebrews 1; 1

Romans 10:17

James 2:15-17

Mark 9:23

Luke 12:48

Jeremiah 29:11

Psalm 37:25

Psalm 1:3

Hebrews 10:35-36

Matthew 18:2-4

Matthew 19; 26

Luke 1:37 (Amplified)

Chapter 5
Becoming a True Worshipper: Fulfilling God's Creative Purpose

John 4:23

John 4:21-24

John 4:23&14:17

Romans 12:1-2

Ephesians 5:19

1Corinthians 10:31

1Samuel 16:13

Psalm 63

Psalm 51

Psalm 63:6-7

Philippians 2:10-11

Rev 5:11-12

Chapter 6

The Abundant Life; Obedience and Victory over Sin

Romans 7:17-25

Galatians 3:2-3

Romans 6:4

Hebrews 4:15

Philippians 2:8

Luke 6:46

John 14:15

John 14:15

John 15:9-10

1John 2:3-5

1Samuel 15:22

Deuteronomy 30:19

Deuteronomy 28:1-2

Colossians 3:3

Galatians 3:26-29

Isaiah 1:19

Chapter 7
Welcome Holy Spirit: My Friend, Advocate, and Revealer of Truth

John 7:37-39

John 14

John 16:14

Hebrew 9:14

Luke 1:35

Psalm 139:7

1Corinthians 12-7-11

1Corinthians 2:10, 11

Ephesians 4:30

Chapter 8
Loving the Way God Loves

Psalm 136

Ephesians 3:18

1John 4:9-10

Romans 8:38-39

John 13-34-35

1John 4:14-20

Matthew 22:37-40

Mark 12:28-34

1st Corinthians 13

Chapter 9
Living for His Glory

1st Corinthians 2:16

Isaiah 11:12

2nd Corinthians 4:6

Matthew 5:13-16

John 14:9-11

John 17:1-5

John 17:20-23

Selected Reading

1. Bound, E.M; The Essentials of Prayer
2. Copeland, Gloria; God's Master Plan
3. Faith's Meaning by Chris Helga do
4. Missler, Nancy; Reflection of His Image: God's Purpose For Your Life
5. Murray, Andrew; The Prayer Life
6. Murray, Andrew, The Master's Indwelling
7. Piper, John; Worship God
8. Ritenbaugh, Richard T, God's Master Plan
9. Tozer, A.W & James Snyder; The Purpose of Man: Designed to Worship
10. Ward, David; Worship: The Christian's Purpose, Privilege and Pleasure
11. Wells, Bob; Proving the Existence of the Holy Spirit
12. Ever Increasing Faith by Smith Wigglesworth
13. Womack, Andrew; Walking by Faith

Notes

Notes

CPSIA information can be obtained at www.ICGtesting.com
Printed in the USA
BVOW020239090911

270749BV00001B/2/P